Presented to:

_____

With Love from:

_____

A LITTLE BOOK OF
Thanks—for Mom

JOYCE VOLLMER BROWN
ILLUSTRATED BY STEVE BJÖRKMAN

Published by J. Countryman, a division of Thomas Nelson, Inc,
Nashville, Tennessee 37214.

Designed by Left Coast Design, Inc. Portland, Oregon

ISBN: 14041-0056-3

www.thomasnelson.com
www.jcountryman.com

Printed and bound in the United States of America

Dedicated to my mother and
all of the incredible, loving,
godly moms like her.

For being my loudest cheerleader through sunshine and through rain; for cheering me up when I failed and cheering me on when I tried again...

Thanks, Mom

For encouraging me to compete against myself, to work at being *my* best without worrying about being *the* best...

Thanks, Mom

For saying "Yes" more than you said "No"…

Thanks, Mom

For knowing when to be tender and when to be tough; for being flexible about things that weren't important and inflexible about those that were...

Thanks, Mom

For making me eat carrots, peas, and broccoli until I liked them and for making me go to Sunday school and church until I wanted to…

Thanks, Mom

or talking to me about Jesus and for talking to Jesus about me...

Thanks, Mom

For warm, gooey chocolate chip cookies and long heart-to-heart talks...

Thanks, Mom

For always being available, for never taking a vacation from mothering, and for never considering your work finished…

Thanks, Mom

For teaching me that friends share everything from lunches to feelings and take turns at having their say and having their way...

Thanks, Mom

For making my friends feel welcome even when they tore up the lawn, left finger-prints on the walls and made tracks on the carpet...

Thanks, Mom

F or telling silly, corny jokes and for laughing at mine...

Thanks, Mom

For letting me fingerpaint, decorate cookies, and build forts in the living room (for encouraging creativity even when it was messy)...

Thanks, Mom

For teaching me to walk, ride a bike, and drive a car...

Thanks, Mom

or teaching me to tell time—and to make the most of it...

Thanks, Mom

or earning my respect, but giving me your love for free…

Thanks, Mom

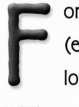

For loving me like no one else does (except Jesus), and loving Jesus even more…

Thanks, Mom

For giving me everything I needed, but not everything I wanted…

Thanks, Mom

F

or giving me fewer things so you could give me more time and for teaching me that the most precious things in life aren't things...

Thanks, Mom

For having a lap that was the nicest, comfiest spot in the world...

Thanks, Mom

For magical kisses that banished hurts and fears...

Thanks, Mom

or all the hours of sleep I cost you when
I was a restless baby, a sick child, and
a dating teenager…

Thanks, Mom

or always seeing me as a promise and a possibility—rather than a problem...

Thanks, Mom

For hugging instead of hollering when I'd wandered off and put you through eternal minutes of terror...

Thanks, Mom

For keeping me safe from the time I was a helpless babe in your arms to the day you let me go and asked God to hold me in His…

Thanks, Mom

For answering thousands of "how" and "why" questions with the wisdom of Solomon and the patience of Job...

or giving me incredibly wise advice—and allowing me to disregard it; for letting me make poor choices so I could learn to make good ones...

Thanks, Mom

or loving me when I was rude,
thoughtless, irritable, and selfish…

Thanks, Mom

For smiling through junior high music programs and games with a score of 10 to 0...

Thanks, Mom

F

or leading and guiding without pushing...

Thanks, Mom

or encouraging me to dream big dreams and to believe Jesus and I can do anything...

Thanks, Mom

For convincing me no problem or request is too big for a God Who created the Milky Way and a multitude of other galaxies…

Thanks, Mom

or reminding me that the size of my faith isn't as important as the size of my God…

Thanks, Mom

For planning, packing, and paying for week-long vacations and then answering "How much longer" questions all the way there—and all the way home...

Thanks, Mom

F

or spontaneous mini vacations to the park, the movies, and the zoo…

Thanks, Mom

For telling me that good habits are as hard to break as bad ones...

Thanks, Mom

For limiting the amount of television I watched and convincing me that life shouldn't be a spectator sport...

Thanks, Mom

For fancy birthday cakes and parties with silly hats and lots of noise...

Thanks, Mom

For gifts chosen with care, wrapped in bright paper and ribbon, and countless others wrapped only in love...

Thanks, Mom

For cooking thousands of meals, washing thousands of loads of laundry, and driving thousands of miles—taking me where I needed and wanted to go…

Thanks, Mom

For serving and loving like an Energizer™ bunny and for being willing to "wash feet" and give your life away—one hour at a time...

Thanks, Mom

F or creating a home where comfort was more important than style, where there was always room at the table for one more plate, and where the most treasured possessions were precious, not because of what they cost but because they were irreplaceable…

Thanks, Mom

For teaching me to enjoy truly great music (like "Jesus Loves Me" and "This Little Light of Mine") and for giving me an appreciation for quality literature and a love for the Good Book…

Thanks, Mom

For thinking I was adorable even when my hair was matted with food, my smile was full of holes, and my face was covered with blemishes...

Thanks, Mom

For filling the house with the smell of cinnamon and roast turkey on Thanksgiving and turning our kitchen into a cookie factory every Christmas...

Thanks, Mom

or always introducing me with pride in your voice and a smile on your face...

Thanks, Mom

For understanding when it just wasn't "cool" to be seen together in public...

Thanks, Mom

or new clothes on Easter Sunday and for telling me how Jesus died so I could become new...

Thanks, Mom

For 4th of July picnics and fireworks
and for teaching me to give thanks
for my freedom in January through
December…

Thanks, Mom

or teaching me that nothing lasts longer than a memory and for giving me a patchwork of tender memories to keep me warm whenever the world feels cold…

Thanks, Mom

For teaching me to ask "What next?" instead of "Why me?"...

Thanks, Mom

For your cheerful attitude and defiant optimism that filled our home with sunshine, even on cloudy days…

Thanks, Mom

For teaching me that happiness is a choice, happiness is a habit, and happiness is often homemade...

Thanks, Mom

or notes, cards, and letters signed with X's and O's...

Thanks, Mom

or teaching me to talk—and teaching me to use important words like "Please," "Thank you," "I'm sorry," and "I love you"…

Thanks, Mom

For explaining difficult math problems, quizzing me on my spelling words, and listening to my book reports (over and over)…

Thanks, Mom

For teaching me to balance a checkbook, shop for bargains, and follow a budget; for teaching me to manage money rather than let it rule over me...

Thanks, Mom

or all the times you let me "help" you when I was little (even though it made the job twice as long)...

Thanks, Mom

For teaching me that anything worth doing is worth doing poorly until I can do it well...

Thanks, Mom

For all the times you helped me by not helping—making me clean my room, wash dishes, and take my turn with the laundry...

Thanks, Mom

For teaching me whatever work I do is divine work when I mentally sign God's name to it—and try to make Him look good…

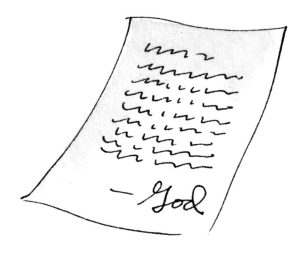

Thanks, Mom

For not shipping me to Australia when I pestered, tattled, and whined...

Thanks, Mom

For not running away to Australia when your "to-do" list  was as thick as a New York City phone book and I balked at pitching in…

Thanks, Mom

For telling me that older folks' memories are some of the finest libraries available…

Thanks, Mom

For daring to be open, to share your needs, to admit your mistakes, and to let me watch you learn and grow…

Thanks, Mom

For teaching Sunday school seven days of the week...

Thanks, Mom

For words of wisdom that still echo in my mind whenever I stand at a crossroads in life…

Thanks, Mom

For being there for so many of my "firsts": my first tooth, my first haircut, my first day of school, my first crush, my first job...

Thanks, Mom

For being the first person I want to share my good and not-so-good news…

Thanks, Mom

For forgiving me: (1) for wanting something every time you sat down or picked up the phone, (2) for drowning the fancy dinner it took two hours to cook in ketchup, (3) for looking in a refrigerator full of food and complaining there was nothing to eat, and (4) for returning your car with a pint of gas in the tank...

Thanks, Mom

or granting me grace again and again: helping instead of criticizing, forgiving instead of blaming, and telling the truth in a gentle way...

Thanks, Mom

For remembering lunch money, overdue library books, permission slips, my turn to bring treats, the carpool schedule, and every friend and relative's birthday...

Thanks, Mom

or knowing the names of my closest friends, the type of books I like to read, my clothes and shoe sizes...my favorite color, movie, and breakfast cereal...and all of my hopes and dreams...

Thanks, Mom

or praying for my friends and their influence on me and for my whole generation and the type of world they'd create…

Thanks, Mom

For teaching me that living in the present is the best way to live for eternity...

Thanks, Mom

For sharing your insights, convictions, helpful hints, secret recipes, and Mother's Day chocolates...

Thanks, Mom

For imparting motherly wisdom passed down from generations, including:

(1) Always try a "no thank-you" serving.

(2) Keep your gum in your mouth.

(3) Tell the truth—it's easier to remember.

(4) A smile is the easiest way to improve your appearance.

Thanks, Mom

For teaching me that words are like toothpaste—once they're out, you can't put them back...

Thanks, Mom

For being a Super Mom who could read my mind, see through walls, do five things at one time, and fly to my side whenever I needed you…

Thanks, Mom

For modeling gratitude: counting what you have instead of complaining about what you don't and never discounting blessings just because they've become commonplace…

Thanks, Mom

or having an irrepressible laugh, a contagious faith, and an inimitable style...

Thanks, Mom

or really meaning it when you tell me to "have a great day" and really listening when you ask how my day was...

Thanks. Mom

For being a sentimental softie who keeps old baby booties, locks of hair, discarded toys, Christmas ornaments made from macaroni, report cards, graduation programs, and newspaper clippings. . .

Thanks, Mom

For nursing me through cuts and scrapes, bumps and bruises, colds and flu…for soothing my hurt feelings and wounded pride…and for mending broken dreams and a battered heart…

Thanks, Mom

For being a great teacher, nurse, coach, counselor, nutritionist, cook, housekeeper, economist, chauffeur, loan officer, historian, and friend...

Thanks, Mom

For your undaunted, unwavering, unbounded, unconditional, irresistible, irreplaceable love…

Thanks, Mom

For: _____

_____

_____

_____

_____

_____

_____

_____

_____

Thanks, Mom